GOD,
PEOPLE &'
THE THINGS AROUND IT

Alonzo Jackson

GOD,
PEOPLE &
THE THINGS AROUND IT

*Putting God first, taking care of your household
and providing for your family and protecting them*

· ALONZO JACKSON ·

REDEMPTION
PRESS

Originally published by Tate Publishing. Re-published by Redemption Press.
PO Box 427, Enumclaw, WA 98022
Toll Free (844) 2REDEEM (273-3336)
www.redemption-press.com

Published in the United States of America

ISBN: 978-1-68314-295-9

Contents

1 Life 7

2 God 13

3 People 23

4 Important Things 31

5 Kids and Marriages 35

1

Life

Sometimes life can be overwhelming, stressful, and challenging. Sometimes we wonder why, why is it happening to me? Well, that's the same thing I ask. Life is not easy and never will be. You just have to take it one day at a time and hope for the best. You can't just wave a magic wand and *poof!* Think things will be all right. Ha ha! Think again. We all seem to get mad when things don't go our way and feel as if it is someone else's fault. That's not right. You can't blame others just because you are having a bad day. Let me talk about work for a second. Work sometimes upsets us. It seems like you might be that one person in your department that goes above and beyond. You stay late, always on time, never call out, and give 100 percent performance each and every day. Well, do you get angry when you're not recognized for your work? Frustrating isn't it? Sometimes we get big responsibilities and no reward. Tell me why every place of work has a person they favor the most? You would think, as a professional place of work, everyone should be treated equally, right? Sorry you had to hear it this way, but it doesn't work like that. Life is never fair. Have you ever had that one person in your department or at your place of work, where every one pulls his or her weight and that one person who never does his or her part? It's not fair when you have to do the work of two people. What makes it even worse is when they know the person is not a good worker, and no matter how many times you say something, nothing gets done about it. Then you work like crazy and someone still has something to say. They know you're a good worker, and they expect you to be the "golden one"—the one who can make any and everything happen. Tough luck. This can really make your life miserable, and sometimes you have to say enough is enough. Try your best to be nice about it and deal with it. A person can only take so much to a point where they say, "I am done". As much as you would like to leave or quit, you know that you can't. You might be the one with kids, a single parent, or whatever the case might be. Temper is a bad thing; your temper can do more bad than good. For instance, it can cause you to be tired to the point that the company you departed from makes it that no one will hire you. My advice to you is to just take a deep breath, count to ten, or do whatever it takes for you to stay calm. If you're a smoker, go outside and smoke a cigarette or whatever you have to do. Perhaps, even take a lunch break. I'm not just writing this for you, I am writing this for myself also. No one is perfect, and no one will ever be. We all have flaws, but these are things that can be fixed. Just hang in there and stick it out. My question to you is, are you ready to accept life as it is? Can you handle life and deal with the things that may come your way? The best way to handle a tough situation is to take it one on one, face it, look it in the eye, and say I will not be defeated and you will not make me upset. By reading what I have written so far, hopefully, you are ready now. I pretty much have accepted it and am ready to move on with my life. Life is too short, enjoy it while you can. Help your kids understand this as well. Glad I could help you stay focused.

2

God

I'm pretty sure you have heard this as one of the things you do not talk about. People, don't get bent out of shape. I'm not about to discuss the Bible or preach to you, I just want to discuss certain situations. I hope you enjoy what I am about to say. No one is raised to say I am a Christian; I was born this way. Think again. No one is born to be anything, it is what you work hard towards becoming. I know we work hard to get the things we have: a nice house, reliable car, great job, etc., which are all nice things to have. As a kid, I was taught at an early age, how to work and make money. My parents taught me how to be a responsible human being. I'm a country boy, who, as a child, had to wake up early every morning before the crack of dawn. My sister and I would work on a farm and feed the animals, change their water, care for them, etc. Did I like getting out of my bed early every morning? You guessed it right, No! Think again. However, as time progressed, my sister taught me to be thankful and thank God for the little work you are doing now. Even though I did not make much money, I was determined to learn all that I could. As a child, my older sister spoiled me and my little sister. Every school year, she made sure that my little sister and I had everything that we needed. She bought our school supplies, clothes, and made sure I always had a fresh haircut. She also made sure that we both had clean clothes and that we didn't go to school with anything dirty on. Same goes for my little sister, she made sure she kept her hair done and a manicure or pedicure if necessary. I thank God for my sister for helping my mom and dad out. As we all know, school can be very expensive, especially when there are still little ones going to school, ranging from kindergarten to fourth grade. I learned at an early age how to accept the little things in life. I didn't care too much about name brands like Nike, Adidas, Puma, and all that fancy stuff. I was thankful just to have something nice and clean on my body. My sister always told us that you don't have to spend a lot of money just to look good. She was right. Back in the day, when the Arizona brand was well-known, I had every new matching Arizona outfit that was out there.

I used to go to school and constantly get compliments about how nice my clothes were. I was even often asked where did I get my clothes from. That really stuck with me. I was like "wow"! Little did they know, they weren't even that expensive. For some reason, people who saw my sister and I just assumed that we wore the most expensive clothes. My point to you, as I said before is, be thankful for the little things and not worry so much about the big ones. As time passed by, I came to love feeding the animals. I actually thought it was cool. I enjoyed it so much to the point that

I used to get up before my sister did. I was just happy to have a job and be able to make my own money. Now that I'm a grown man, something my sister said to me still resonates with me. She said, "Alonzo, this will help you in the long run." She was right. I used to get mad at my parents when they did not give me money to go to the movies, buy a new shirt or whatever the case might have been. I'm glad for the lessons my sister taught me. And thanks to her, in high school, I worked two jobs and still went to school. I learned several ways to make money while in school as well. I would sell chips, drinks, candy, and basically whatever I could to earn money. However, instead of using that money on myself, I used to try and help out with the bills or at least put something towards them. Being determined at the time, I figured why not start now trying to become independent. The more I worked and made money, the more I was able to continue to help out. I thank God for my parents raising me to be the hardworking young man I am today. We, as Christians, sometimes forget the importance of God and what He has done for us. One day India, a friend of mine in my biology class, invited me to go to church with her. She told me her church was having "Friends Day," and she wanted me to come. As time drew closer to that day, not knowing how to pray or really what to say, I closed my eyes and said, "God, thank you for everything. Thank you for blessing me with a family that loves me dearly. God, please help me to not let any distractions get in the way of me attending 'Friends Day' watch over me in Jesus's name, amen." So now it is the day to attend church for "Friends Day." I was a bit nervous at first, but India helped me to relax and stay calm. We got to church, and everyone there was so nice and welcoming. They treated me as if they had known me for a long time.

I really enjoyed myself and had a great time at church. India and her brother Mike has been going to church for a while now. From that point on, I was at church every Sunday and Wednesday. I was raised in the church, in which I had relatives who were preachers, deacons, ushers, etc. As a child, I would go to different churches, and it was quite an experience. I guess I was looking for that perfect church to become a part of. But something hit me and I realized that there is no perfect church. As long as you are obedient to God, you shall be blessed. Trust me, I have had my fair share of attending different churches. First Assembly of God was the church where I felt God wanted me to be. I was a member of that church for five years and it felt good to be a part of it. During those five years, I became really active in the church and participated in many activities. Those activities ranged from being on the drama team to playing on the church softball team. The pastor at the time received a promotion and had to leave us. That was one of the saddest days of my life. So we had to find another pastor to come in and preach the Gospel to us. Several months had passed since the other pastor left and we finally found another pastor to take his place.

Now, I know that when some people hear the word *church*, they push away from it. Church is a wonderful thing, and God died on the cross for our sins.

3

People

Like I was saying in chapter 2, people hear the word church and some people push away from it. I come to you today, my friends, to say that I used to feel the same way about it. I used to get into all kinds of trouble by hanging out with the wrong crowds. Being a teenager, I felt like I had to be cool. I felt I had to do what others were doing just to fit in and that it was the right thing to do. Guess what? I started getting into so much trouble. My parents worked hard to make sure I had what I needed. I took advantage of it and didn't listen. I was hard-headed but never missed a day of school. I even went to school on the days that I was sick. So, you know all of that changed right? I started skipping school and thinking I was doing "cool" things knowing it was wrong. My friends and I would walk down the highway like everything was good. Just our luck, here comes a police officer driving down the street, saw us and made a U-turn in the middle of the highway. The officer stopped us, got out of the car, and asked us why we were not in school. All we could do was just stand there because we were at a loss for words. The officer then made us get into his vehicle. He asked us, "So what school do you all go to?" To which we replied, and then he proceeds to call our school. He talked to the principal and told the principal that he picked up a few students; they were skipping school and walking down the highway.

The officer asked, "Do you want me to bring them to school?"

The principal replied, "I wasn't even aware that any of my students had been doing that."

Guess where we ended up going? The officer took us straight to the detention center. All I could think about was, *Why did I do what I did? Why did I not listen to my parents?* So we got to the detention center and went inside. We were then told to take our clothes off and empty our pockets out. Next, they made us put on jail suits while they proceeded to call our parents. We then were placed in a holding cell. We were told to sit in that holding cell until our parents came to pick us up. Hours passed and all the other guys' parents had come to pick them up. I said to myself, "I guess my mom is not coming to get me." As I waited, the correctional officer started walking me around the cell, trying to talk some sense into me. He was helping me understand that I didn't want to be in here. "Enjoy your freedom," he said. It really woke me up and from then on, I learned my lesson. My mom finally came and picked me up, that's what a caring parent does. To this day, I still thank God for blessing me with a loving mom and a family that loves me unconditionally regardless of what I've done wrong. I realized that all the stealing and hanging out with the wrong crowds had to stop. I had to cut ties with all the negative energy, and let go and let God deal with me. I knew I had backslid tremendously, but I knew I had to move forward. That night before I went to bed, I got down on my hands and knees and said, "Lord, I know I have done a lot of wrong things and have not been obedient to you, nor my parents and for that I'm sorry. God, please help me to stay out of harm's way, help me to do right by you, in Jesus's name. Amen." God heard my cry, answered my prayer, and took care of me. I got back into church and a few months later, I was baptized. The story gets better; not only did I get baptized, my mother and my sister did as well. At the time, I really didn't understand what it meant. I knew this is what I had to do though because God said so. So my point is, we as people who have good-paying jobs, nice cars, and nice houses, oftentimes don't tell God thank you. Well, we are all guilty of this. We say, "my this" or "my that", but we never take the time out to say, "thank you, Lord, for my job. Thank you, Lord, for all the things I have. God, you are the reason I have this." Remember, God is the key to all of our success. All our blessings come from the Lord. The more I stayed in church, the more I realized how powerful God is. He brought me out of a hard situation. I knew if it wasn't for God protecting me and watching over me, I would have not been here today writing this powerful message.

I understood the importance of tithes, the more I gave the more I received. All kinds of blessings started coming my way. I was blessed with not one, but two jobs. So of course, the more I made, the more I gave. God began to do things in me to reach out to those in need and help people. My mom always told me to treat people the way I would want to be treated, and she was right. She also said, "Son, always help people because you never know when you might need help." God blessed me with a promotion at my first job. God even took it a step further and placed my second job right up the street from the other. Anyone could tell you that this was definitely a blessing from God. I was that person that if you came to my job and you didn't have all of the money to pay for your items, I would give you the rest of the money to pay for it. If I was at a gas station and someone needed gas, I would have given them gas money. If I saw a homeless person and I had food in my car, I would feed that person. So my advice to you is to always accept God. Do not go a day without thanking Him. Give your offering like I did. You will and should be blessed. Keep the faith, and He will take care of you, my friend. God is good to us all.

4

Important Things

This topic was one that I had to pray about. I didn't really know what I wanted to name this chapter nor this book. God spoke to me and said, "Name this book *God, People & the Things Around It*. This book will be about the things we face in our everyday lives. We all have had to deal with life; therefore, we know that every day is a challenge. I believe in order to deal with these obstacles, we must be humble and stay focused. The world we live in today is a crazy place. So many things happen each and every day that are beyond our control. Do you ever ask yourself, "Is the world coming to an end?" Well, I think we all know that one day it will happen. We do not know when nor the hour, but will you be ready? Here's my advice to you: Accept our Lord and Savior Jesus Christ, try to find a church home and be washed in the water to be baptized. Trust me, I know life is not perfect. No one lives a perfect life. That's just not going to happen. That doesn't mean that we can't be born-again Christians. Do God's work and be laborers for Christ. Reach out to friends, family, and coworkers and let's make this world a better place.

Like my mom told me, "you only have one life to live. Enjoy it and be glad in it." There are a lot of important things in life we should all remember. Number 1: Put God first in your life and be faithful and obedient. Number 2: Take care of your family and love one another. Now I know there may be some family members that you may or may not get along with, love them anyway. Love is the most powerful gift there is. God sees that, and He will help pave the way for you and yours. I know everyone as a teenager coming up dreamt of one day having a family of their own. It's a wonderful thing to desire and who wouldn't want that? Personally speaking, I have been there and done that. I have two boys and a stepdaughter whom I love dearly. I went through a lot as a young adult, not knowing what I wanted to do in life. You know what? God brought someone into my life, which at first, she didn't like me. Her siblings did the best they could to play matchmaker, but nothing seemed to work. As time went by, after constantly trying to win her over, she finally gave me a chance and she fell in love with me. They say that good things come to those who wait. All I had to do was stay humble and be patient.

5

Kids and Marriages

As I stated in the last chapter, God blessed me with a special someone whom I felt was the one for me. Guess what? It lasted for a while. A total of about nine years. We dated about four and a half years and was married for about the same length of time. Things were great in the beginning and we were doing so well together. Everyone thought that we would be together forever, including me. Well, so much for that thought. I think that's when I learned the lesson that nothing is promised to last forever. It's what you make out of it. God blessed me with two wonderful boys whom I love so much. My wife, at the time, and I both worked two jobs. We did what we had to do to take care of our kids. It wasn't easy, but we knew in order to give our kids what they wanted and needed, that it was necessary. After working two jobs for what seemed like a long time, I decided that I wanted to go back to school. I wanted to be able to support my family better and spend more time with them by establishing a career.

I started looking at different schools and finally found one that looked promising. The decision was not at an easy one at all. I stepped out on fate and decided to enroll into the school. This meant that I had to move to a different state and leave my kids behind, which is something I didn't want to do. I always traveled back and forth about twice a month, sometimes every two weeks to see my kids. Unfortunately, things didn't work out in my marriage and I filed for divorce. I am a firm believer of not divorcing, but when you have done everything in your power to save a marriage and it still does not work out, then it's time to let it go. But before the divorce occurred, I did come back for my kids and wife at the time. By that time, I had my own place and brought my family to where I was living and going to school. I knew that in order to save my marriage and not tear my family apart, we had to be together as one. By me being the man of the house, I knew that my responsibility was to be there for them at all times. We were a happy family again, and I was able to take my kids to the park, go out to eat, and do other things that a normal family would do. Whatever my kids wanted to do, I was there and did whatever I could to make it happen.

Just as things were getting good, a shocker happened. My wife, at the time, had a family emergency and had to go back home. Guess what? She took the kids back home with her. That was a really sad day for me. Not having my kids around me each and every day hurt me deeply and almost depressed me. I would go to the park and see kids and their families, and I would say to myself, "This is nothing but the devil." It never fails, whenever you try to do the right thing and be there for your family, a roadblock occurs. Being the man I was,

I felt like I wasn't a good father because I did not have my kids with me. My biggest fear was feeling like my kids hated me. I did not want my kids to think that I was a bad father in any form or fashion. Later on, my wife and I, at the time, had gotten a divorce. Due to her infidelity, it caused our family to separate. I tried to save our marriage, but it could not be saved. It hurt me so much because our kids did not ask to be in this world. I can assure you that the saying is true in regards to children in a divorce. They say that when you have kids from a marriage and the parents separate, the kids always suffers in the end. I never intended for that to happen to them. I love my kids dearly and I will do whatever I can to take care of them. Being the father that I am and continue to be, if I were to walk into a store right now and my kids wanted something, I would spend my last dime on them. I want to give my kids all of what I didn't get the chance to have when I was a child.

I thought that after the things I went through, despite the divorce, that I would be afraid to love again. As hurt as I was, it took me a while to get over it. Eventually, I did though. Thanks to my lovely mom who said, "Son, I know you are hurt, but you must move on with your life." What I am trying to say is that sometimes we think that just because we are with someone, or have kids by someone, that we have to stay with that person. Maybe even continue to be with that person. I prayed every day that one day I would be able to find someone whom I could spend the rest of my life with. Guess what, my friend? God answered my prayer. I knew that I had to be patient and wait on Him. I found a new church to attend due to a friend of mine from the school I went to. I met a nice woman who loves the Lord as much as I do. She loves and cares for my kids like they were her own. I thank God for bringing this special person into my life. Since then, things have gone well for me. So with that being said, no matter what happens in your life, whether or not you get divorced, find a special someone, or get remarried, just know that everything happens for a reason. Never say never and you must stay strong and fight for what means a lot to you. Because I've endured these things, I can truly say that life has never been the same again.

Order Information

To order additional copies of this book, please visit
www.redemption-press.com.
Also available on Amazon.com and BarnesandNoble.com
Or by calling toll free 1-844-2REDEEM.